Stage and §

M000031706

15 Simple Steps on How to Stage and Sell Your Home – Fast!

Every year homeowners miss opportunities to make more money by not taking a little extra time and effort to stage their home and make it more attractive to buyers.

In this revolutionary Itty Bitty Book, Eduardo Mendoza shows you how to use his proven, easy-to-do tips and low cost techniques to design a more beautiful home that everyone wants to buy – now!

Immediately start using these simple but effective 15 ideas and tips in your home today and you will be amazed at how easily your house stands out from the rest on the market and attracts people ready to buy.

For example:

- Make your bathrooms look like spas
- Create spaces that feel comfortable and inviting to potential buys
- Design rooms that help your home sell for over the asking price

Pick up a copy of this easy-to-use book today and you'll see just how easy and fun it is to stage your house and how happy you'll be from the extra revenue that comes when you sell the home quickly.

Your Amazing Itty Bitty™ Sell Your Home Book

15 Simple Steps on How to
Stage and Sell Your Home – Fast!

Eduardo Mendoza

Published by Itty Bitty™ Publishing
A subsidiary of S & P Productions, Inc.

Copyright © 2015 Eduardo Mendoza

All rights reserved. No part of this book may be
reproduced or transmitted in any form or by any means,
electronic or mechanical, including photocopying,
recording or by any information storage and retrieval
system, without written permission of the publisher,
except for inclusion of brief quotations in a review.

Printed in the United States of America

Itty Bitty™ Publishing
311 Main Street, Suite D
El Segundo, CA 90245
(310) 640-8885

ISBN: 978-1-931191-88-3

Table of Contents

Introduction

Step 1.   Front Door

Step 2.   Entryway or Foyer

Step 3.   Living Room

Step 4.   Kitchen

Step 5.   Dining Room

Step 6.   Powder Room

Step 7.   Master Bedroom

Step 8.   Master Bathroom

Step 9.   Hallway

Step 10.   Guest Room

Step 11.   Kids' Rooms

Step 12.   Closets

Step 13.   Basement

Step 14.   Exterior Façade

Step 15.   Garage

Stop by on the Itty Bitty™ website to find interesting blog entries regarding staging and selling houses.

www.IttyBittyPublishing.com

For more information or to reach Eduardo, please visit

www.theenhancedhomestaging.com.

Introduction

It can be an exciting time when you decide to sell your home but it can also be stressful trying to figure out how to make your house look its best in order to get the most value when it's sold.

The visual appearance of your home is extremely important and plays an essential role the moment the first potential buyers walk through the front door. People begin judging your house within the first few seconds of looking at it, so it is critical that you put your best foot forward. Your home also has to look lovely and desirable in photos taken for sales fliers, real estate websites and videos.

Decorating your home for your personal taste and enjoyment is one thing, but when you need to sell your home, you need a different perspective. You need to design and stage the home to appeal to other people. You are using your home to sell a certain lifestyle that is fresh, neutral and welcoming so that it appeals to potential buyers with a variety of tastes and styles. They need to feel comfortable in the home and easily imagine making it their own if they buy it.

That's where staging comes into the picture. Staging is a simple and effective way to show off your home's best features and make it look more spacious and inviting. The process goes beyond just touching up the paint, putting away the clutter and baking some cookies to make it smell good. When done right, the staging process helps not only make your home look great, but can help it sell more quickly and make you as much money as possible.

Here are some interesting facts about staging:

- 95 percent of staged houses sell in about 10 days compared to 90 days for non-staged properties.
- Nearly 1/3 of sellers' agents say staging raises a home's value by 6 to 10 percent.
- Almost half of all agents say buyers who see a staged house online are more likely to visit.

I've collected many staging tips over the years and I'm happy to share them with you in my book. Each chapter has up to five different, easy-to-read tips to help make sure your home looks and feels as beautiful as possible – and sells quickly!

Thanks so much for reading and happy staging!

Eduardo Mendoza

Step 1
Front Door

First impressions are everything. The minute a potential buyer walks up to your house, you want them to feel "at home" and welcome. There are a number of things you can do to make the entry to your home feel welcoming and inviting.

1. Make sure the front door looks as pristine as possible. The paint or stain color should be fresh and free of chips or scratches.
2. Frame both sides of the front door with two large pots of greenery or seasonal flowers. Reflect the part of the country you live in by using local, seasonal plants. This will add some warmth to the entry and break up the concrete or brick that is often used in walkways up to a house.
3. A new, clean, simple black doormat or one made of sisal will give you the most value. Avoid using doormats with messages or images.

Visual Suggestions On How To Present the Exterior Door/Façade of Your Home

Step 1.

- Front Door Colors (1)

    http://goo.gl/hJsUYD

- Front Door Pots (2)

    http://goo.gl/eBKojb

- Front Door Mats (3)

    http://goo.gl/od5c0r

Step 2
Entryway or Foyer

You know what it feels like to walk into a grand hotel lobby? You get that instant sense of luxury and comfort. That's the goal for your entry hall or foyer. You want your potential buyer to enter your home and immediately feel welcome and want to stay and relax. How you decorate and style this space is crucial for enticing people to want to come in and look around further.

1. Save the best piece of art you have in your home and place it in the entry. This will be the first thing seen and the buyer's first impression when entering your house.
2. Make sure the wall paint is perfect and there are no old nail holes in the wall.
3. If you have space, bring an appropriately-sized table and vase of flowers into the foyer. If the table is wood, use a porcelain vase and flowers of all the same color to have a cohesive look.
4. Clear the room of all clutter in the entryway. This includes things like piles of running shoes and boots, purses, backpacks and umbrellas. You don't want this entry space to look like a dirty mudroom.

Suggestions for Items That Look Appealing in an Entryway or Foyer

Step 2.

- Entry Wall Art (1)

    https://goo.gl/3faz91

- Entry Table (3)

    http://goo.gl/oSP5sr

Step 3
Living Room

The living room is often seen as the heart of the home and it is important to stage it properly. You want to give the sense of a comfortable place where friends and family come together to have fun. You don't know if your potential buyers like to watch movies with a big bowl of popcorn or host elegant cocktail parties. You need to create a space with comfortable seating and ambiance to help them imagine the possibilities.

1. Start with the basics; a typical living room usually consists of a sofa, two armchairs, a coffee table, and a rug that frames the room and keeps all of those furniture items together.
2. Keep the room simple, while incorporating a few different design elements. For example, if your sofa and chairs are solid and chunky, use a more "leggy" coffee table with elegant lines.
3. Even if you have the most stunning view in the world, don't face the furniture toward the window or deck. It needs to help people imagine connecting inside the room with friends and family.
4. Keep the top of your coffee table clean and simple. You only need a few design elements, like a large vase with real or synthetic white flowers and two, stacked coffee table books. Try to have a cover of a book that shows a beautiful image, like a vacation spot or interior of a room.

Suggestions for Decorations on Coffee and End Tables

Step 3.

- Living Room Furniture (1)

  https://goo.gl/QfKff6

- Living Room (3)

  http://goo.gl/8STC0c

- Living Room Coffee Table Arrangement (4)

  https://goo.gl/klWLh8

Step 4
Kitchen

Kitchens are important spaces in homes where people often come together to share meals and to entertain. You want yours to feel clean, fresh and healthy. One of the best ways to do this is by making the right choices when you design your kitchen countertops.

1. Be sure to keep the countertops as clean and clutter-free as possible. Put away all small appliances, including things like toasters, blenders and coffee makers. Show as much counter space as possible.
2. To help potential buyers envision using the space for cooking, put just a few, decorative details on the counter tops. Add a small container with a few wooden spoons and a whisk near the stove. On another part of the counter, place two or three large glass jars filled three-quarters of the way with colorful things like yellow pasta, green lentils or red beans.
3. On an island or a corner of the counter, place a large bowl filled with the same kind of real or fake fruit, like bright green apples. It is important to make sure the bowl looks full.

Suggestions for Items to Decorate Your Countertops

Step 4.

- Kitchen (1, 2, 3)

    https://goo.gl/e2VXOY

Step 5
Dining Room

A dining room should feel like a wonderful place to share meals and conversation with friends and family. It might also be a space that invites people to sit and linger over a cup of coffee while reading the morning paper or gather around the table to stay up late laughing, while playing board games. Everything from eating delicious, healthy meals to having fun, are the feelings you want your dining room to express.

1. The dining room table should be the appropriate size and scale for the rest of the room and sitting space for six is ideal. For example, a large dining room with a small table and just two chairs wouldn't be a good choice.
2. If you have a wood table, to make the look more interesting, look for another material when it comes to your chairs. Try something different like chairs covered in leather or a fabric, or even chairs made out of a hard plastic. Everything doesn't have to match perfectly. Mixing leather or fabric with a wood table adds warmth to the room.
3. Choose a centerpiece that is an appropriate size and scale for the table and that also adds a mixture of texture. If the table is glass, try using a vase of a contrasting material like wood, with a lovely flower arrangement.

Visual Suggestions on How to Present Your Dining Room

Step 5.

- Dining Room (1)

  http://goo.gl/Tb3sTT

- Dining Room (2, 3)

  https://goo.gl/LI1QvJ

Step 6
Powder Room

This is a room that might be small, but can still make a big impact on a potential buyer. Most important for all bathrooms in your house is that they are clean and convey a sense of tranquility. With just a few simple touches, a powder room can easily become a beautiful space that helps enhance your home.

1. A powder room should have some pizzazz. This is where you can have some fun and personalization in your décor. For example, you could hang a piece of art that compliments the colors of the walls.
2. If you have counter space, put a simple white orchid or other white flower in a white pot. If counter space is limited, for a more sophisticated look, use a pretty and fresh bar of white soap with a pleasant scent.
3. If there is a bar for a hand towel, as well as a bath towel, be sure to use a plush, white towel. You want one that will be wrinkle free so it shows up well in photos and looks good to potential buyers.

Suggested Items That will Give Pizzazz to Your Powder Room

Step 6.

- Powder Room (1, 2, 3)

    http://goo.gl/PKTAYv

Step 7
Master Bedroom

This is an important room that needs careful attention to detail when staging your house. Everything from the way the bed linens are made to the number of accent pillows is important in making sure this room looks clean, spacious and elegant, and conveys a lifestyle that is relaxing.

1. Every master bedroom should have a full, queen or king-sized bed – the right size for the room. There should be two nightstands, two table lamps, and if room allows, an armchair to show seating.
2. You want the master bed to be made as crisply as possible so it looks clean and fresh, like a hotel. Start with sheets in a solid color and then top them with a quilt. If you want to add another layer, fold a duvet in a different color into thirds and lay it across the foot of the bed.
3. At the head of the bed, you should place four pillows of all the same size. The two back pillows can match the color of the sheets and the two in the front can match the color of the duvet cover, if different. In front of the four pillows can be one complimentary decorative pillow if you choose.
4. If you have a TV in the room, be sure to remove it. You want to convey a sense of peacefulness and relaxation, not Sunday night football and the news! Use the TV space to place a piece of art that sends a message of peaceful sleep or romance.

Other Suggestions for Accents in the Bedroom

Step 7.

- Master Bedroom (1, 2)

    https://goo.gl/Ml46oS

- Master Bedroom (3)

    https://goo.gl/kRWWl3

Step 8
Master Bathroom

As with your master bedroom, it is important that when people walk into your master bathroom they instantly get a sense of feeling clean and fresh. It needs to be relaxing and spa-like in every way. Keeping things crisp and simple will go a long way to make the room appealing.

1. Always use white, plush, fabric shower curtains and white towels. This will make the room feel open and clean.
2. Black and white art is best, and images and pictures that convey the fresh outdoors are ideal. Images and photos of the ocean, sand and beach shells are always good.
3. Rid the counters of clutter and add a white orchid contained in a white pot. That will make the room feel like a spa.

Suggestions for Items to Decorate the Master Bathroom

Step 8.

- Master Bathroom (1)

  http://goo.gl/8KuQZJ

- Master Bathroom (2)

  http://goo.gl/1ti7Mn

- Master Bathroom (3)

  https://goo.gl/BlFlNK

Step 9
Hallway

It doesn't matter how many hallways your home has, they all need to be open, well lit and approachable. Although these transition spaces are intended to help people move between the rooms in your home, they also play a role in creating a cohesive feel and help add to the look of a well-staged house.

1. Hallways tend to be narrow. One way to make the walkway space feel larger is to add a mirror at one end. Another way to bring in some color and still keep the hallway simple is to add a gallery of art pieces lined up in a row. They should all be the same size and hung at the same height (the center of the art should always be kept at eye level).
2. If you have a floor runner in the hall, make sure there are at least three inches between the rug and the wall on each side. If not, remove the rug because it can make the hallway seem too small.
3. Keep all hallway doors clear of posters and art. They should be clean and the color of the doors should match the color of the trim.

Visual Suggestions for Hallway Decorations

Step 9.

- Hallway (1, 2, 3)

  http://goo.gl/vlGCWD

Step 10
Guest Room

To most potential buyers, an extra bedroom is a big plus. It conveys a sense of spaciousness for their future guests, children or they even might have plans to turn it into a library or office. It is important for you to keep the décor simple and focus on staging it as an elegant second bedroom that gives a sense of purpose, but let's them keep their options open.

1. The guest room can get a more simple design treatment than the master bedroom. In addition to the bed, if the room is large enough, include two nightstands and two small table lamps. If there isn't room for the extra furnishings, try using just a floor lamp on one side of the bed.
2. To make a guest bed, use the same technique as you did in the master bedroom, but this time, just use two matching pillow cases and one small decorative pillow.
3. You can be a bit more creative and personal in this room. If you choose to decorate the walls with some interesting art or photographs, try to incorporate colors that you used in the bed linens or that are in the wall color.

More Suggestions for Decorating a Guest Room

Step 10.

- Guestroom (1, 2, 3)

  https://goo.gl/Q1FHMz

Step 11
Kids' Room

This is definitely a room where you can have fun with your staging and show a little personality! That said, it is best if it isn't overly baby-focused and decorated in all pink teddy bears. It is important for this room to just convey a sense of youth and playfulness for a young boy or girl.

1. Bedding can be used in any primary color and the decorative pillow can include any creative kid theme like the ABCs or a giraffe, or comic books or sports.
2. Just like the guest room, a full or queen-size bed is ideal and a floor lamp is fine. If a twin bed is used, try to have a small nightstand and playful lamp design.
3. It is easy to think small when staging a room for kids. Keep in mind that any art used to decorate a room for kids still needs to be big enough to show up well in photographs.

More Suggestions for Decorating Kids' Rooms

Step 11.

- Kids' Room. All three things that I am suggesting on the previous page are contained in this picture.

  https://goo.gl/vCieU4

Step 12
The Closets

Closets are sometimes forgotten when it comes to staging, but they can make or break a home sale. When they open up your closets, you want potential buyers to see well-organized and brightly lit spaces, not piles of junk and boxes of clutter. If you take a little time to make sure your shelves are clean, it will definitely pay off.

1. To make a closet feel as large as possible, be sure to remove all items from the very top of the shelving.
2. Nothing should be on the floor, so put things like shoes and purses up a bit higher on shelves.
3. Group all clothing together, first by type (pants, shirts, long coats, etc.). By keeping the hanging length of these items the same, the closet will feel more organized. Then you can organize them by color.
4. Not all of your hangers need to match. And be sure to leave some open hanging space to show prospective buyers that there is room for their clothing. The closet shouldn't look too packed.
5. Avoid painting a color inside the closet; white walls are all you need. Color sometimes makes a closet feel too dark and small.

Suggestions for Aids to Organize Closets

Step 12.

- Closets (1, 2, 3, 4, 5)

    https://goo.gl/yWFKP0

Step 13
The Basement

An unfinished basement can be presented as a potential space for all kinds of options to prospective buyers. They might want to turn it into anything from a laundry room, to a home gym, to a playroom for the kids. You want to do whatever you can to present this room as clean and organized and give them a sense of possibilities.

1. The best way to present a basement is by painting the ceiling and walls bright white and the floors either light grey or beige. If cables or pipes are exposed, paint those white, grey or beige, too, so they match and aren't distracting.

2. If there is built-in shelving and you are storing things in this space, keep everything in concealed moving boxes. Clear plastic boxes might help you find things, but they show your mess to potential buyers.

3. Try to keep top shelves empty to make the room feel more open. The closer boxes are to the ceiling, the more it creates a feeling of being cramped and might make it harder for your potential buyers to envision space for their own boxes.

Suggestions for Basement Ideas

Step 13.

- Basement (1)

  https://goo.gl/Qjg4vr

Step 14
Exterior Facade

The exterior curb appeal of your home can be just as important as the inside of the house. No matter how nice the interior photos of your home look online or in a flier, if the outside of the house looks old, dirty or unsafe, potential buyers will drive on by.

1. Your landscape should look fresh and well maintained. Replace any trees, shrubs or plants that are damaged or look unhealthy.
2. For a fresh first impression, power-wash the roof and clean all gutters of leaves and other debris.
3. If your exterior paint looks chipped or outdated, it is worth considering power washing or even investing in a fresh coat or even a modern new color.

Visual Suggestions on How Your Façade Should Look

Step 14.

- Facade (1, 2, 3)

    https://goo.gl/XFrLlW

Step 15
Garage

A garage is an important feature for many potential home buyers, so you don't want to forget about this space. Like the rest of your home, it is important that it is staged well and looks clean and organized. You want it to be fairly empty to help the potential homeowners envision using it for whatever they need, from car storage to a wood-working shop.

1. Make sure the garage looks like a garage. You should leave enough empty room so the potential homeowners can envision parking at least one car; if the garage is large, two is ideal.
2. Nearly everything should be removed from the garage to convey a sense of spaciousness. The best things to leave in a garage are a few gardening supplies and tools.
3. Just like an unfinished basement, the ceiling and walls should be painted a bright color like white, grey or beige and the floors should be painted to match.
4. While it might be appealing to store unused furniture and household items in the garage, invest in a storage unit and put these large, bulky items in there while you are trying to sell the home.

Suggestions for Garage Ideas

Step 15.

- Garage (1)

    https://goo.gl/fY512i

You've finished. Before you go…

Tweet/share that you finished this book.

Please star rate this book.

Reviews are solid gold to writers. Please take a few minutes to give us some itty bitty feedback on this book.

ABOUT THE AUTHOR

Eduardo Mendoza is an interior design expert and has been designing and staging spaces in homes for over 10 years. As a nationally recognized home stylist, he specializes in the art of redesign: reconfiguring existing furniture, art and décor in the best way possible.

His work has been featured in national media outlets around the world, from Asia to India, to Latin America to the U.S. They include Forbes, Univision, Zillow, and Seattle Homes and Lifestyles.

He is originally from Lima, Peru. His multi-cultural experiences bring an international perspective to his work with individual homeowners, realtors and developers. He studied residential design at the Art Institute and combines professional degrees in business and hotel management with his education and experience in the interior design world.

For more information or to reach Eduardo, please visit http://www.theenhancedhomestaging.com.